D1385201

KEEPING IT SIMPLE

Perhaps you've been captivated by the impossibly colored gems in your dealer's tank, or maybe you've gained confidence in your aquaristic skills with a few freshwater tanks and are looking forward to the challenge of a saltwater one. Then again, maybe those tanks you've been passing up for years with the reasoning that you could buy a whole tankful of tetras for the price listed for one saltwater fish might now show individual prices that aren't all that different from a tetra's. Perhaps since you've kept some scats or gobies or some other brackish water inhabitants, you realize that the dividing line between freshwater and saltwater fishes is not so clear. Whatever your reason for considering a marine tank, you could not have picked a better time to start one.

First of all, the marine hobby, once reserved to the elite few who had mastered the chemistry and had the tenacity and the financial means needed to pursue this branch of the aquarium hobby, is now open to virtually anyone interested in it. While it appears that some marine aquarists spend more time measuring redox potentials and monitoring ion concentrations than they do watching their fishes, it is possible, thanks to that same

Today the equipment and knowledge available to beginning marine hobbyists make it possible for them to create tanks rivaling the one shown here in good looks and faunal diversity.

PHOTO BY U. ERICH FRIESE AT JEM AQUATICS.

Monodactylus argenteus, one of the popular tropical fish species that finds itself at home in both freshwater and marine aquaria.

PHOTO BY EDWARD TAYLOR.

modern technology, to set up a marine tank that is fairly simple to maintain. And, because of the increase in interest in marine fishkeeping, there are now many inexpensive products available for the hobbyist that were unobtainable at any price just a decade or two ago.

Additionally, the price of many marine fishes is now much more within reach of the average hobbyist. The concern about reef-damaging cyanide trapping, plus improved methods of shipping and handling fish, have resulted in lower mortality rates, which, of course, means lower prices. I myself was hooked when I visited a pet shop that had some freshwater cichlids (which were reasonably priced and over which I would not hesitate a moment) bearing higher prices than the fishes in a tank of assorted saltwater damselfishes.

While the maintenance of an invertebrate reef aquarium is right now at the cutting edge of marine technology and rightly the domain of knowledgeable, experienced hobbyists, the trickle down (pun intended) of expertise and products that enable the captive reproduction of a microcosm of a tropical coral reef full of invertebrates has also given the marine fish hobby a wealth of knowledge and equipment to simplify and to enhance the keeping of marine vertebrates as well.

Are you ready for salt water? You're taking the right first step in reading books like this one, in getting the information you need to make your initial foray into the marine hobby a successful one. If you have the desire and are willing to arm yourself with practical knowledge before you set up that tank, you are likely not only to succeed in keeping such a challenging and rewarding aquarium but also to go on to increase your marine tank space.

All of the experience you've gained with freshwater tanks will carry over into saltwater tanks. Granted, a few things, like salt mixes and specific gravity, are not part of the freshwater hobby, but all of the basic principles of freshwater aquarium management exist for marine husbandry as well. In the following chapters we will discuss setting up your first marine tank.

We will be talking about establishing a very simple and inexpensive marine collection. Just as you got your feet wet (pun again intended) slowly with freshwater fishes, you should start out slowly with saltwater fishes. You can save the more difficult species (and the higher price tags) for later on, but you won't be sacrificing the excitement of a marine tank, nor will you have to forgo the sparkling beauty, since many of the hardiest and least expensive marine fishes are among the most colorful.

You may have heard of the **KISS** anagram, which has several variations, some of them rude, but for us here it is: **K**eep **I**t **S**imple (at the) **S**tart. This book is centered around the principle of keeping it simple in order that you can maximize your success with the minimum of confusion and a reasonable amount of effort.

From the very beginning, one of the best resources you can have is a knowledgeable, helpful tropical fish dealer. He or she can provide you not only with sound advice and help with problems but also with high-quality fish, since an experienced dealer will be selling healthy, well-acclimated livestock. Your dealer is a natural **KISS** filter, able to distill from all the products and procedures what you need now and what is best kept for later. Dealers who believe the best way to succeed is to inform their customers and to sell them only what the customers actually need will not have you waste your money on useless gadgets and doo-dads or talk you into buying products beyond the scope of your initial attempt at saltwater, nor will they sell you incompatible fishes, fishes that won't eat, or fishes that won't live out the week. In other words, they **K**eep **I**t **S**imple at the **S**tart.

With marine fishes as with freshwater tropicals, good looks don't always have to be accompanied by high prices. Some of the most brilliantly colorful of marine tropicals, such as the damselfish species *Chromis cyanea* shown here, are among the most reasonably priced.

THE TANK ITSELF

Years ago, when the lack of knowledge and technology made everything concerning the marine hobby difficult, the best salt water to be had was carried from the beach in a bucket, and people had rows of black and white marbled tanks punctuated by an occasional shiny-new stainless steel one. The first advice to the beginner back then was about using only stainless steel tanks for salt water and of coating all exposed metal with epoxy to keep it from contacting and reacting with the briny spray. Today, with precisely engineered artificial salt mixes and the ubiquitous all-glass aquarium, the first advice to prospective marine aquarists usually centers on the size of the tank.

While it is true for both freshwater and saltwater tanks that the larger the aquarium, the more forgiving it (and its inhabitants) will be of mistakes you make, for marine tanks it is doubly so. The natural marine environment is a much more complex and stable one than freshwater lakes and streams; the marine *aquarium*, on the other hand, is potentially a terribly unstable environment, one lacking in many of the natural buffers and controls that, while adding to the complexity, also preserve a safe, hospitable, unchanging environment for its inhabitants. Thus when we're talking about a saltwater tank, instead of the bigger, the better, think: the biggest, the best.

The absolute minimum for a beginner is a 20-gallon aquarium, and a 30-gallon or more would be preferable. This is not to say that even the smallest aquaria cannot be used for marine setups, but they should only be attempted by experienced saltwater hobbyists. Even if it seems counterintuitive to you, it's true that the larger the tank, the simpler its care—and the easier time you will have of it.

The extremely popular 48-inch-long 55-gallon aquarium is a good choice, and these tanks are often available in a special package deal with full hood and reflector at a most reasonable cost. Such a tank is large enough to give you some leeway until your husbandry comes up to speed. In addition, marine fishes must be stocked at rates considerably lower than those for their freshwater cousins, and many beginners can't bring themselves to keep a tank with only two or three fish in it. The 55-gallon lets you have a little more variety and still stay within safe limits.

The popularity of this tank stems from its proportions for viewing the aquarium contents. Unfortunately, the tall, thin design, so aesthetically pleasing, is not in the best interest of the inhabitants of the tank. The factor that determines the carrying

Setting up marine aquarium, especially a mini-reef tank like the one pictured, requires an aquarium of decent size. Don't start off with too small a tank, because tanks very restricted in water capacity are very unforgiving of the type of mistakes beginners often make.

PHOTO BY MP AND C. PIEDNOIR.

capacity, or stocking rate, of an aquarium, all other things being equal, is not the volume of the water but its surface area, since that is where the gas exchange takes place. The absolute volume of water is a factor in the ability of the tank to accommodate pollutants and store oxygen, but only for an extremely limited time. It is foolhardy to rely on mere volume to preserve water quality, since the "size" of an aquarium depends on how you measure it.

For example, the four-foot-long 55-gallon tank has a surface area of about four square feet. The squatter three-foot-long 50-gallon aquarium, on the other hand, has a surface area of about four and a half square feet, so the "smaller" (in gallons or length) tank is "larger" (in surface area)! A 75-gallon tank, with the same front glass dimensions and viewing area as a 55-gallon, has a surface area of about six square feet, a 50% increase over the 55-gallon, but this is the same surface area as a 90-gallon tank, which is simply taller.

Surface area is the reason many people advise against the popular hexagon aquaria. These tanks, however, are perfectly suitable as long as you realize that you cannot put anywhere near the number of fish in them as you could in a standard tank of the same gallonage.

There is nothing "wrong" about any size or shape aquarium. As long as the constraints of the tank are understood, you can select any tank you want, but you must concern yourself with the surface area and respect the limitations of the tank you choose.

As with any other setup, the tank must be placed on a solid, level surface, preferably on a commercially built stand designed for the particular tank you have. That filled 55-gallon tank will weigh in at around 600 pounds, so you have to be sure the floor you place it on can take the strain. Stands with four solid sides rather than a top rim and legs are preferable in this regard. If all of the tank's weight is supported by four legs with one-inch diameter feet, the total is borne by just over three square inches of floor, for a pressure of almost 200 pounds per square inch for a 600-pound load. The same load borne by a continuous perimeter rim $^3/_4$ in. wide goes down to not quite seven pounds per square inch.

The tank should be away from temperature extremes such as doors, windows, heating and cooling vents, etc., and it should be situated where you can enjoy and service it as you go about your daily routine.

Proximity to a drain and faucet for water changes and a *ground fault protected* electrical supply should also figure into your choice of location for the tank. That last is important enough to stress by repeating that you'd never use your blow dryer in the shower; well, you should never plug any aquarium appliance into any outlet which is not protected by either a ground fault interrupting (GFI) receptacle or a circuit covered by a GFI circuit breaker. This is one technological product that is mandatory even in a **KISS** system, where we can redefine the anagram as "Keep It Safe (and) Survive." Unlike oil and water, water and electricity unfortunately *do* mix, with inevitably disastrous results. This is just common good sense, and the pennies saved by ignoring it could never make up for the potential loss being courted by such negligence.

SALT WATER

Obviously, the water you use in a marine tank will be salty, but how do you get it that way? If you're used to hatching brine shrimp, you may wonder if you could just throw some kosher or solar salt into the tank. If you live on a coast, you may imagine how much money you will save by using ocean water for free instead of buying salt mixes, and even if you've already decided to use salt mixes, you are probably wondering which one to use and whether that really makes a difference. Let's consider these one at a time.

No, you cannot use pickling salt, kosher salt, or water softener salt, the way you can to hatch brine shrimp. You probably *could* keep some species of marine fishes alive for a day or two in such solutions, the way you do the brine shrimp, but your goal is to keep them alive and healthy for

The artificial marine salts being made today are the products of years of experience and study and completely suitable for setting up and maintaining even delicate fishes and invertebrates. Photo courtesy of Coralife/Energy Savers.

a long time. Natural seawater contains almost every element in some form, at some concentration, and while a sodium chloride solution begins to approximate seawater, it falls quite short of it. To hatch brine shrimp you can use brine shrimp solutions, but to keep marine species, you need seawater.

Now, while you beach-dwellers might think that natural is the best way to go, the simplest as well as the cheapest, you should reconsider. Unless you are reading this on some pristine uncharted Pacific isle, the water along the coast is polluted. All of the chemical and physical debris that mankind dumps into the ocean is most concentrated near land. You might be able to pick out the larger bits of sewage and assorted flotsam, but you can't remove the organic solvents, pesticides, fertilizer residues, petroleum seepages, and all the other garbage we've littered the seas with.

The seawater mixes available today are the result of an enormous amount of research by marine scientists, who have formulated various mixes for the optimum health, growth, and livability of the captive organisms we wish to keep in our aquaria. Water you just scoop out of the ocean is of unknown composition. Also, that water you scoop up is, of course, natural. So, what's wrong with that?

Plenty. Ocean water is not sterile; it is teeming with life. Even a bucketful of what seems to be just water is full of viruses, bacteria, and myriad varieties of minute plants and animals. Almost all of those living things in the seemingly empty bucket of seawater are not going to survive in the closed system of your aquarium. A few are actually going to bloom frantically in the absence of natural controls, but very shortly they're all going to die, and their decomposition will put a fatal overload on your biofilter (which, if you're just setting up the tank, won't even be functioning yet). Getting natural seawater ready for use in an aquarium is an involved task, either of storage and decanting or of chlorinating and dechlorinating. When you consider the pollutants, uncertain composition, and bioload of natural seawater, you have the three strikes necessary to call it out. Play it safe (and easy) and use artificial mixes. They really are the choice of the **KISS** setup.

Okay, so which one? Once again your dealer can assist you in that choice. All of the leading brands are fine to use; at this point, as a beginner, you

A range of products designed to condition water and supply it with trace elements, provide protection against stress, prevent diseases and keep the marine environment clean and healthful is available to saltwater hobbyists. Photo courtesy of Tropical Science.

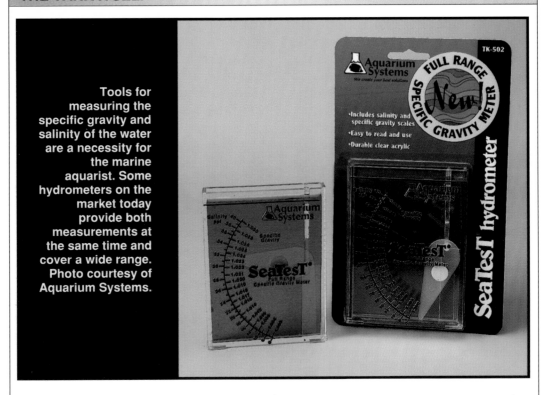

Tools for measuring the specific gravity and salinity of the water are a necessity for the marine aquarist. Some hydrometers on the market today provide both measurements at the same time and cover a wide range. Photo courtesy of Aquarium Systems.

shouldn't be concerned about the small differences among them. By getting your supplier's advice you will get a brand that is stocked by the store, a brand that your dealer knows to be a quality product, and, quite likely, the brand the fishes you'll be buying there are already used to.

All quality mixes today are nitrate- and phosphate-free. Should you locate a bargain mix that is not devoid of these two ions, avoid it like the too-good-to-be-true mistake it is. Unless, of course, you wish to have an algae-only tank, in which case you can salinate and fertilize at the same time.

So now you've picked out your salt mix. The salinity of water is measured by either parts per million (ppm) or specific gravity, which is a measure of the density of the water as compared to pure H_2O, which has specific gravity of 1.000. Oil is less dense, a hunk of lead is more dense, and salt water is more dense than fresh water.

You probably couldn't detect the slight weight difference between a bucket of fresh water and a bucket of salt water. The difference is vital to your fish, however, and it marks the physiological differences between marine organisms and other aquatic life.

Body fluids have a higher specific gravity than fresh water but a lower specific gravity than sea water. This means that freshwater fishes are faced with an osmotic problem of always taking on water into their cells, since water flows across membranes from an area of lower concentration (the lake) to the area of higher concentration (the cells of the fish's body). They need to excrete excess water and hang onto their body salts. Marine fishes have the opposite osmotic situation—they are always losing water from their tissues into the sea around them. These fishes have to take in water all the time, excreting excess salts, and they are in constant danger of dehydrating their body tissues. The habits, kidneys, and gills of fishes all reflect this situation, and the understanding of this difference only makes one wonder how brackish water species, many of which will do well in both fresh and full salt water, as well as in various mixtures of the two, manage to survive!

Thus a reliable hydrometer to measure the specific gravity is an absolute necessity, since it is the resultant specific gravity of your aquarium water with which you are concerned, not the precise amount of salt to add. You will want to make a mix that reads between 1.020 and 1.025 at aquarium temperatures.

Okay, we've discussed the salt, and how much to use. What about the water? If you use tap water for your freshwater tanks, it might seem appropriate to do the same for your marine tank, but it is not advisable.

Why? Since most tap water comes with a host of chemicals, mostly minerals, already dissolved in it, when you use it as a basis for artificial seawater you wind up, in effect, adding all those minerals to the carefully researched and formulated makeup of the mix. Having paid good money to get a properly balanced salt mix, you throw it off balance with the tap water. Reverse osmosis (R.O.) water or distilled water is much better for your purposes, since they are virtually devoid of any dissolved substances. Such pure water, when mixed with the salt mix, yields exactly the composition seawater that the scientists who formulated the mix intended, and which your fishes need to thrive in your care.

Once again, what looks like a complication, using water other than tap water, turns out to be the simpler choice, and free from the worries the simpler-looking choice entails.

OTHER EQUIPMENT

Once you've decided what size tank you want and where you are going to put it, it's time to consider the other equipment you'll need. The list is not carved in stone, and some hobbyists insist on a piece of equipment that other equally successful hobbyists wouldn't be caught dead with. Keep in mind that your goal, at least at first, is to make as stable an environment as you can for your fishes while still keeping things simple; there will be time to fine-tune your marine husbandry later. Live sand, live rock, R.O., ORP, VHO, Berlin system—it's easy to get lost in all the terms and technology, so you'll be much more likely to avoid frustrating failures if you remember to **KISS**.

There is nothing wrong with

The type of equipment, especially filtration-related equipment, you'll need is determined partly by the size of your aquarium and also to some extent by the type of animals you're going to keep in it. An aquarium containing both fishes and a wide variety of invertebrates, as this one does, is going to require a greater degree of sophistication in its equipment than a fishes-only aquarium would.

PHOTO BY PHILIP HUNT.

saltwater setups that have as much or more room devoted to the filtration system as they do to the aquarium itself, but your first attempt at saltwater fishes doesn't have to be that complicated. Likewise, you should not let current debates regarding aquarium setup deter you from starting in the hobby. Yes sand or no sand? Yes UGF or no UGF? Yes this or no that? The reason these debates exist is that there are no concrete rules about marine aquaria, and for every attempt someone makes to issue one, there is at least one experienced hobbyist who disproves the "rule" by the successful practice of its opposite.

FILTRATION AND AERATION

Let's start with equipment you're already familiar with. Circulation and aeration are, of course, also concerns of the marine aquarist. In fact, since salt water cannot hold as much dissolved oxygen as fresh water at the same temperature, aeration is even more important in the marine tank. Air pumps, power filters, and powerheads are all useful for this purpose, as they are for freshwater tanks.

Likewise, the three types of filtration you are already familiar with have their place in the saltwater system. The use of mechanical filtration media such as polyester fibers, gravel, or woven filter pads traps suspended particles and keeps the water clean. Outside power filters or canister filters are widely used to provide this type of filtration in saltwater tanks. Remember, though, that until you clean the filter medium, the garbage is still in the water flow, even if it is located outside the aquarium, and it continues to feed bacteria or to leach substances into the water the same as if it were still in the tank. Clean the filters often, and as always, remember that frequent water changes and siphoning of the substrate are major contributions to water quality.

Vacuuming the substrate is equally important. This should be done regularly, even daily. While a thorough job is ideally coupled with a regular water change, smaller interim cleanings can consist of siphoning debris out of the gravel and straining the water through some filter medium, then returning it to the tank. Or use one of the power filters that have gravel vacuuming attachments, but, again, remember to change the medium afterwards, otherwise you have done only a cosmetic cleaning. Any water loss from siphoning must, of course, be made up with salt water, but daily topping off of the tank's loss from evaporation should be with distilled or R.O. water, since the salt is left behind when the water evaporates.

You're undoubtedly familiar with chemical filtration using carbon. Many marine aquarists use other chemical filtration media in addition to activated carbon, and they tend to use more expensive, higher grade carbon than their freshwater peers. The sensitivity of marine organisms to chemical pollutants in their water makes it doubly important to keep the water as free from invisible dissolved contaminants as from cloudiness and sediment. The desire to prevent algal blooms motivates the use of the higher grades of carbon, which are more efficient and are free of phosphates, as well as various resins that remove selected contaminants. For your first **KISS**

The aquarium housing this colorful starfish and other invertebrates not only looks beautifully clear and clean but also is relatively very free of dissolved waste products of all kinds, all as a result of the efficiency of filtration techniques and equipment available today.

PHOTO BY U. ERICH FRIESE.

tank, you can rely on quality carbon and regular water changes to maintain water quality.

Canister filters are the common location for chemical media in saltwater tanks, but regular power filters can also be used. Because of the initial dangers of pollutant buildup in newly established tanks, it is wise to fill filters exclusively with carbon at first. When the carbon is due for replacement (follow your dealer's and the manufacturer's recommendations), you can refill the canister with a variety of media if you wish.

The different types of biological filtration probably get more attention in the marine hobby than any other type of water quality control. Let's take a brief tangent here. This is one of those areas in which you must not let the plethora of data, divergent scientific viewpoints, and conflicting advertising claims overwhelm you. You will hear about dozens of filters, special maintenance systems, computer-controlled monitoring systems, and wonder products that let you go years and years without changing water. This is not the forum to debate the pros and cons of all this technology. As you grow in the hobby, you will become familiar with the high tech options open to you, and you will be able to discuss them with people who have tried them and make up your own mind.

In keeping with our **KISS** plan, I make this simple observation: if you follow the recommendations here, you will have a successful start in the marine hobby, as thousands of others have. If you choose to go a different route, you should make sure that you really understand the technologies you select before you even fill the tank with water.

So, back to biofiltration. The undergravel filter (UGF) is the quintessential **KISS** device. A perforated plastic plate, an airstone or powerhead, a tube or two, and you have an efficient biofilter. Marine hobbyists swear either by or at the UGF. Why? They are inexpensive, easy-to-use, and quite efficient, but they are also prone to clogging, inclined to trap wastes under the plate, and subject to total tank tear-downs for cleaning. A bit of history will put things in perspective.

Before the nitrogen cycle and biofiltration were understood, marine fishkeeping was a risky art. The UGF brought scientific reliability to the saltwater hobby, and it was quickly elevated in people's minds to a position it could hardly live up to. Thus, as people began to experience problems and failures with this miraculous piece of technology, two things happened. Its reputation became sullied, and people looked to alternative biofilters. So what's the truth about these filters?

The UGF permits the myriad particles of the substrate in

the tank to function as colonizing sites for the bacteria necessary to convert ammonia to nitrites and nitrites to nitrates, and it supplies them with the required constant supply of oxygenated water. Various problems, however, can arise.

Areas of the gravel or plate can become clogged with debris, cutting off the circulation in that area. This not only stops the biofiltration in that spot but also permits anaerobic bacteria, which flourish in the absence of oxygen, to thrive. These unfriendly bugs produce toxic substances like hydrogen sulfide, which bubbles up from infected gravel when it is disturbed.

Also, since detritus is pulled down into the gravel bed, it is not removed and continues to decompose, lowering oxygen

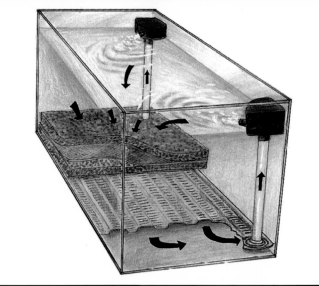

Illustration showing the basic operation of a regular (that is, non-reverse flow) undergravel filter. The arrows show the direction of water movement.

DRAWING BY JOHN R. QUINN.

levels, raising pH, increasing dissolved nitrogenous wastes, and providing food for bacteria that are not welcome in the tank. When sufficient gunk accumulates in the gravel and under the plate, you have to take the whole tank down and clean everything out.

There are ways around each of these problems, however, which stay within the **KISS** boundaries; with one or two exceptions, the alternative technologies do not.

There are two ways to prevent both clogging and waste accumulation under the plate. The first is to refrain from overfeeding and to keep the substrate as clean as possible. You can do this by employing a powerful outside filter while keeping the water flow through the UGF at a low rate. This enables the power filter to trap most of the suspended dirt before it is sucked into the gravel. You will also be siphon-cleaning the substrate with each water change, if not more often. By agitating the gravel with a suction tube, particles that have begun to percolate down through the bed will be sucked out with the water to be changed. In addition, the tank tear-down can be postponed or even eliminated by occasional vacuuming *under* the filter plate.

How? Remove the airstone or powerhead from each lift tube. Slide a piece of tubing slightly less than the diameter of the lift tube down until it hits bottom. Lift it slightly and siphon. You can use a simple gravity siphon, but if you attach the tubing to a water pump and suck the trapped wastes out under power, you will get better results. Remove the tubing, replace the airstone or powerhead on each lift tube, and you're done. One total tank tear-down avoided.

Incidentally, if you have the tank where you can look under it at the bottom glass, you can tell when you need to clean under the plate, and, while you're cleaning under there, keep track of your progress.

The second method of circumventing the problems with a UGF is to refrain from overfeeding and to use a reverse flow UGF. In a reverse flow setup, powerheads are used to pump water *down* the lift tubes, under the plate, and *up* through the gravel. A sponge prefilter on the powerhead means the water pumped through the gravel is free of suspended dirt. Frequent vacuuming of the substrate is still necessary, but you will not find anywhere near as much debris with the reverse flow system, as long as your power filter is running efficiently.

In other words, with a few simple maintenance practices you can enjoy the biofiltration benefits of a well-functioning UGF in your marine tank. Even in today's high-tech world, many successful saltwater hobbyists use these filters as the sole biofilter in their tanks.

I mentioned high-tech alternatives within **KISS** parameters. One is the power filter with a bio-wheel. This technology, like many other aquarium technologies, is adapted from municipal water purification systems and is one of many "wet-dry" designs.

Wet-dry filtration is based on the fact that air contains thousands of times more oxygen than does oxygen-saturated water. By placing a porous or fibrous medium under a spray or trickle of water, the filter provides not only suitable sites for bacterial colonization but also oxygen levels far superior to those obtainable in any submerged system. The "dry" filter medium is in fact wet, but just barely. Covered with only a film of water, the bacteria benefit from the extremely high oxygen concentration of the air while still remaining damp enough to survive. The surface area thus required for biofiltration is considerably reduced from that needed by submerged filters, with a single biowheel providing the

biofiltration of about thirty pounds of gravel.

Such wet-dry filters have other advantages as well. Because the water splashing onto the medium is prefiltered, there is practically no maintenance needed. The medium does not have to be cleaned, which means the bacteria can continue to grow undisturbed.

A power filter with a bio-wheel is, therefore, a valid **KISS** addition or alternative to the UGF. Either, or both, will provide efficient biofiltration and aeration. Many other biofilters, such as trickle filters and fluidized bed filters, are excellent devices, but they are neither as simple nor as inexpensive as the systems we have discussed. The new fluidized bed filters basically take UGF filtration out of the aquarium, eliminating the disadvantages of such a system and optimizing the

Fluidized bed filters achieve a high degree of effectiveness among biological filtration devices by greatly increasing the surface area of the filter medium on which beneficial bacteria can live and by providing the oxygen-rich environment they require. Some fluidized bed filters also allow for a degree of chemical and mechanical filtration. Photo courtesy of Wardley Corporation.

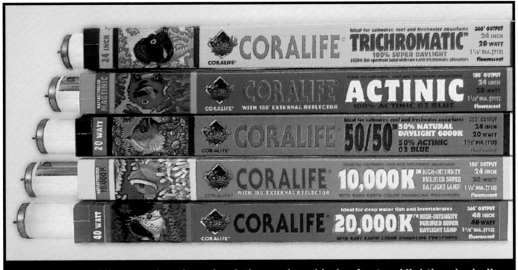

A wide range of fluorescent tubes simulating various kinds of natural lighting, including lighting that would be most beneficial to invertebrates harboring photosynthetic algae, is available at pet shops and tropical fish specialty stores. Photo courtesy of Coralife/Energy Savers.

use of the surface areas of the sand particles for bacterial colonization.

Over the next few years fluidized bed filters will undoubtedly undergo considerable improvements and expansion of features. It is best, perhaps, to leave technical innovations out of a **KISS** until they are proven and refined.

LIGHTING

You have probably noticed the large proportion of advertising devoted to marine lighting systems. You'll see multiple-bulb designs, HO and VHO bulbs, metal halide systems, and prices that will make you think the decimals have been accidentally moved to the right. None of this sounds very **KISS**, and it isn't.

The biggest reason for the concern about lighting in marine tanks is that many saltwater invertebrates, most noticeably the coelenterates (e.g., corals and anemones), require high intensity, full spectrum lighting because of their symbiotic zooxanthellae, which live in their tissues and photosynthesize.

Since you will be starting with a fish-only tank, the only lighting necessary is what you need to properly enjoy the beauty of your fish. A regular aquarium fluorescent fixture and bulb will be fine. Complicated lighting systems are yet another thing you can wait to tackle.

TESTS AND MEASUREMENTS

You're used to making tests and measurements in your freshwater aquarium. You'll need to keep track of the chemistry of your marine tank as well. The hydrometer has already been mentioned as a required piece of equipment. The clear acrylic floating-needle type is quite popular and easy to use; just be sure you don't get any air bubbles in it, or they'll throw off your reading considerably.

Older style glass floating hydrometers that ride higher in the water as salinity increases are also quite serviceable. Whatever type of hydrometer you use, make sure that you read the scale correctly; follow the manufacturer's instructions. You want to maintain a specific gravity of 1.020 to 1.025.

A few test kits can be used in both fresh and salt water, but many cannot. Make sure the kits you use are suitable for saltwater testing. You will find a large variety of test kits for checking everything in your salt water from pH to copper and iron concentrations, from calcium ion concentration to O_2 saturation. So, which do you need?

You should obtain and use the saltwater equivalents of the hardness, pH, nitrite, and ammonium tests that you would use on a freshwater tank. A nitrate test kit is also a good idea, to let you know how effective your water changes are. Under the **KISS** plan, for a fish-only tank, these tests should suffice. The total hardness and carbonate hardness should be high; keep the pH above 8.0, ammonia and nitrite levels as close to zero as possible, and nitrate levels low.

Good salt mixes are buffered, so hardness and pH are rarely a problem at first. The tank's pH, however, can drop drastically and dramatically when the tank is overstocked, the fish are overfed, or the filtration systems are over-relied on and the power goes out. As the pH falls because of the presence of acidic byproducts of decomposition, the oxygen level also drops. You should therefore check the pH daily, at least until your biofilter is established and you are used to the maintenance of your tank.

One other familiar and necessary device that needs no explanation is the thermometer. Remember that one of the ways that the ocean is more stable than most bodies of fresh water is in its temperature, which does not experience the wide variation that streams, rivers, and ponds undergo. The tank's temperature should be monitored constantly, so a reliable thermometer should be a permanent part of the setup. This brings us to the last familiar piece of equipment and to a related but more specifically marine one.

TEMPERATURE CONTROL

Most marine tropicals are best kept at 75° to 80 F°, so a reliable heater is a necessity. The acceptable temperature range is narrow because of the stable nature of most marine environments. Influences such as change of season, rainy periods, flooding, and solar heating can drastically affect the temperature of bodies of fresh water. Marine organisms, except for a few specialized creatures such as estuary or tidepool inhabitants, are not exposed to this type of variation. That is why the marine

Invertebrates such as the disk anemones and gorgonians thriving in this tank are sensitive to changes in temperature, but it's not so much a small change in temperature itself that hurts them as an *abrupt* change.

PHOTO BY U. ERICH FRIESE AT JEM AQUATICS.

hobby is concerned with aquarium chillers as well as heaters.

Chillers are one solution to summertime temperatures, and they come in all sizes and capacities for different-size setups. They are not cheap, even the less expensive ones available for a modest marine setup that needs to bring down the temperature only a few degrees. Another alternative, however, is to air condition the room in which you have the aquarium, giving you, your family and your fish the benefit of reduced summer temperatures.

Remember that salt water, which already has less dissolved oxygen than fresh, loses even more oxygen-carrying capacity as the temperature rises, so extra summertime aeration is extremely beneficial. Evaporation, which can be increased by both adding more aeration and by setting a fan to blow across the water surface, removes a lot of heat from an aquatic system. Just remember to keep the water level up and the specific gravity correct by replacing evaporation with distilled or R.O. water. Excess heat is a concern, but fishes are less susceptible than many invertebrates to overheating, so you do not have to be quite as concerned as a frantic reef hobbyist during a summer heat wave.

PROTEIN SKIMMERS

You won't get far in the marine hobby without hearing about protein skimmers, also called foam fractionators, for good reason. They're simple, effective, and, by most people's standards, essential in any marine tank for the removal of organic pollutants *before* they get a chance to break down. Skimmers significantly decrease the load on the biofilter, and, consequently, they reduce the buildup of toxins in the tank. But if they're so good, why don't you use one in your freshwater aquarium?

The nature of salt water is such that air bubbles foam up more in it. You may have noticed that the airstones in marine tanks seem to put out a much foggier stream of bubbles than those in freshwater tanks. If you watch the bubbles breaking the surface, you will see that saltwater bubbles are smaller and more long-lived; vigorous aeration (including from waves) produces a "suds" you will not see in unpolluted fresh water. This fact underlies the technology of a protein skimmer, which is operated by either an airpump and special airstone or by a venturi to introduce the air bubbles into the water stream.

The skimmer works because many substances, most notably organic compounds, adhere to the surface of bubbles. By forcing a stream of bubbles through a narrow column of water from the tank, many of these contaminants are flushed out as the foam created by the bubbles is skimmed off and trapped in a waste receptacle.

Skimmers come in many varieties; some fit inside the tank, some are external, and others fit into the sump of trickle filters. There are even power filters that incorporate skimmers within themselves. You needn't get fancy. Just select one that is rated for your size tank or slightly larger.

There are two major drawbacks to skimmers. The first, much more of a concern in invertebrate or reef tanks, is that skimmers can remove beneficial substances, such as trace elements, along with the contaminants they so effectively trap. Your regular water changes should offset this problem in your fish-only tank.

The other drawback concerns their being somewhat at odds with the **KISS** principle. Skimmers work only when they are properly adjusted, and you have to practice to get them adjusted correctly. They also need constant

The collection cup of a protein skimmer in operation.

PHOTO BY U. ERICH FRIESE.

maintenance, such as daily emptying of the foam collection cup and rigorously regular replacement of the airstones. In this case, however, two arguments work toward the inclusion of protein skimmers even in a **KISS** system.

First, they are extremely beneficial, especially in a beginner's tank, where conditions might be less ideal than those in an experienced hobbyist's tank. While "they really work!" may not be sufficient justification to call them simple enough for **KISS**, it does persuade.

Second, there is no real alternative. You can avoid the super-colossal-wet-dry-trickle-double-sump-automatic-refill-connected-to-your-pager-clear-acrylic filter that takes up the whole space under the tank and then some and still get a fair replacement in a biowheel power filter that hangs on the back of the tank. The protein skimmer, however, is extremely simple, even minimal, in design and has no close alternative other than a constant stream of new salt water flowing through the tank. While extremely simple and wonderfully efficient, the impracticality and expense of that solution make the skimmer much more attractive to a **KISS** scheme.

A skimmer is not an absolute necessity; people used to keep marine fish without them, and some still do. The odds are much more in your favor, however, if you include this simple accessory. Admittedly, it requires precise adjustment and careful care, but it will make an enormous difference to your fishes and therefore also to you. So get one, read the instructions, ask your dealer for a demonstration and for hints, then set it up. Make only minor adjustments, then wait to see how things are going.

You should not panic and rush to readjust things if you find that your skimmer decreases its output over time. A newly set up system will have much more organic waste than a balanced system with an established biofilter. Also, if you add a skimmer to a tank that has been stocked for some time, you will notice a great decrease after it removes the initial backlog of wastes.

STERILIZERS

Sterilizers get much more attention by marine hobbyists than by freshwater fishkeepers. One reason for this is the need to eliminate microalgae in reef tanks. In addition, marine fishes are more susceptible to infections and diseases than freshwater species, at least more so than those freshwater fishes that have been bred in captivity for decades. Thus the interest in sterilizers. These devices kill microorganisms, clearing up water and preventing disease by attacking the root causes— microscopic creatures.

The two types used are ozone generators and ultraviolet (UV) sterilizers. Both can be dangerous (to you and to your fishes), both are expensive, and both require technical knowledge to maintain them. While the ozone generator is basically a one-time purchase even though it needs considerable regular attention, the UV sterilizer, though fairly easy to keep operating, needs frequent (every six months maximum) replacement of the expensive UV bulb.

You can undoubtedly guess what's coming next—sterilizers are not really KISSable. If the expense is not a problem, UV sterilizers, once installed in a filtration circuit, are simple enough to operate, and as long as you keep fresh lamps in them they provide a real benefit, both in keeping your fish healthy and in keeping the water clear. You should purchase a unit rated for a slightly larger tank than you'll be using, since the output of the UV bulb begins to drop off immediately, and a unit barely ample for your setup will quickly be working below minimum effectiveness. This is one of those pieces of equipment, however, that you can forgo in your first **KISS** tank.

SUBSTRATE AND DECORATIONS

As a freshwater hobbyist, you may be thinking about a planted saltwater tank. Forget it. For the most part, marine plants are not like terrestrial or freshwater plants, which are predominantly higher (vascular) flowering plants. Seaweeds are macroalgae, their "leaves" basically long strings of simple cells similar to single-celled algae.

Macroalgae, especially species of the genus *Caulerpa*, are popular in reef tanks, but they have two major drawbacks for you. One, they are a tasty snack for almost any fish and will be grazed away in no time, and, two, they are definitely not KISSable. Like those invertebrates that incorporate photosynthesizing organisms in their tissues, macroalgae need intense light; they promptly die and foul the tank when they don't get it. If you like the looks of the seaweed you see in your dealer's or a friend's tanks, start saving, both money and knowledge, for your first mini-reef tank, complete with live rock, live sand, and live plants. For now stick with inanimate decorations.

Almost none of the inanimate items you decorate your freshwater tank with are suitable for your marine aquarium, however, being either totally inappropriate or inferior to something else. The major exceptions to this are ceramic or plastic ornaments and plastic plants. Many hobbyists consider these unnatural in freshwater tanks and even less aesthetically suited to saltwater ones, but they are not hazardous. If you like them, use them. Your fishes will avail themselves of the hiding places they provide without worrying about whether they're natural enough.

Driftwood, the natural decorative water conditioner for soft, acid, "black water" tanks, is a definite no-no. The tannins it leaches into the water are alien to any marine environment except brackish mangrove swamps, and their tendency to soften and acidify water is at cross purposes with your highly buffered, hard, alkaline saltwater mix.

When acquiring rocks for your freshwater tank, you were cautioned no doubt about various types suitable only for salt water, such as limestone and coral rock. Now most of the freshwater-safe rocks you are familiar with can be used in saltwater tanks, but, being largely from terrestrial

The same is true for coral or dolomite substrate. Besides looking more like an ocean bottom than quartz gravel, coral sand or crushed dolomite serves to keep hardness and pH at optimum levels in a marine tank. Sand is also the preferred substrate for those fish species that burrow into it and can be inhibited or even injured by coarser gravel.

Coral—that is, the dead, bleached skeletons of colonial

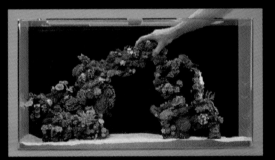

Simulated corals can be built up into impressive structures that provide good looks, shelter and a base upon which algae and invertebrates can grow in the aquarium. Photo courtesy of Ocean Nutrition.

locales (streams, waterfalls, river gorges), they do not look anywhere near as natural in the marine tank. In addition, the soluble minerals in salt water-only rocks help to buffer your water against fatal pH drop.

hard corals— used to be the traditional decoration for marine tanks. Recently the loss of reef ecosystems has focused concern on any harvesting of marine species, and, fortunately for the hobbyist, plastic replicas of many coralline structures are now available. These artificial corals are very convincing, are a snap to keep clean, and usually cost less than the natural models.

You will want to fashion rocks and corals with epoxy or sealant into structures that provide sufficient hiding places to make your pets feel secure enough to act naturally and to provide them refuge from aggression. Other than that, your taste and your budget should be your only guides.

CYCLING THE TANK

So you're all set up. The water is in and at the proper salinity, the filters are running, the lights are on, the skimmer is bubbling away, and the heater is maintaining the proper temperature. Ready to stock it with fishes? No!

The nitrogen cycle must first be started so that the biofilter can begin to grow. Over the years I have seen various proposals for how to do this, from adding one fish at a time over a period of a couple of months to feeding the empty tank as if it had fishes in it, from seeding the tank with ammonium chloride to many others, some more bizarre than promising.

In addition, there are on the market bacterial cultures, specifically made for saltwater systems, that give the biofilter a jump start by supplying a concentration of the appropriate species of *Nitrobacter* and *Nitrosomonas* bacteria. Claims as grand as "add culture, water, and

fish" abound, but although these products can vastly shorten cycling times, you should not rely on them to make the tank instantly ready for a full complement of fishes.

So how do we **KISS** and cycle the tank? Remember, caution can make up for a whole lot of technology. To be safe, add a proprietary culture, one or two fish, feed sparingly for a couple of weeks, and monitor the water. After that time, if the water still tests within acceptable limits, add another fish or two, but keep a close eye on the ammonia, nitrite, and nitrate levels. They should peak and decline in that order over a period of up to six weeks. At that point you can stock the tank to its capacity.

Another alternative is to borrow a biofilter. You can do this by using gravel from an established marine tank that uses a UGF as a substantial portion of the substrate in your new tank. Or you can place several sponge filters in an established marine tank for a month before you set up your tank, then put them in— instant biofilter. Or, if you are using a biowheel filter, you can take the biowheels from an established marine tank and use them on the filter on your new tank. The first and last of these alternatives have the drawback of depriving the old tank of much of its biofilter, but it can work, especially if your new tank is smaller than your friend's established tank, which would let you leave some of the old filter media behind.

FISHES FOR THE KISS SYSTEM

The fishes you choose for your tank will, of course, be dependent on your budget, your preferences, and what is available where you live at the time you wish to set up your aquarium. There are no fishes that you *should* include in your tank. There are, however, quite a few that you *should not* purchase, either because they are not hardy enough for a beginner or because they are not suited to aquarium life no matter how skilled the aquarist is. Unfortunately, fishes of the last type do make it to dealers' tanks on occasion. (Yet another reason to develop a working relationship with a reputable and trustworthy dealer.)

Right now the saltwater hobby is the inverse of the freshwater hobby, which deals primarily with captive-bred fishes, since only a tiny percentage of marine tropicals are bred commercially. In the years to come we should see a repeat of what happened with freshwater species as more and more marine fishes are successfully spawned in captivity and as we get successive generations of captive-bred fishes.

Obviously, any fish not inclined to breed in captivity will not leave

Clownfish like these *Amphiprion ocellaris* are now being bred commercially and offered for sale to marine aquarists at reasonable prices. The availability of fishes that have themselves been spawned under aquarium conditions will make it even easier to breed future generations of captive-bred stock.

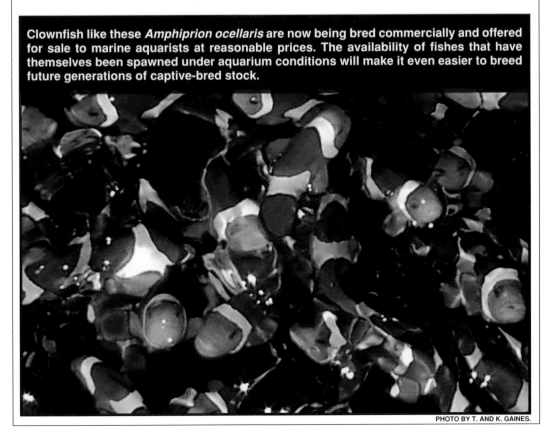

PHOTO BY T. AND K. GAINES.

captive-bred descendants, while those that can be coaxed into spawning will add their adaptability to the captive-bred gene pool. At the same time hobbyists will hone their understanding of their pets' needs and improve their ability to supply those needs.

For years an insurmountable obstacle to breeding success, the fact that most marine fishes have a planktonic larval stage has turned into a challenge that hobbyists and commercial operations are rising to meet. As the methods and the technology improve, captive-bred marine tropicals will be increasingly available. Such fishes are generally more adaptable than wild-caught fishes, and you should choose captive over wild whenever you can.

What follows in this chapter is a listing of hardy marine species suitable for your first few tanks. You can pick and choose as the size of your tank, the scope of your finances, and your appreciation of the different species dictate. You will have to keep their "personalities" in mind when combining them, and, as always, you must not place a fish smaller than another fish's mouth in with that fish. Even strict herbivores cannot resist that temptation! Soon you will want to refer to one of the many excellent atlases of marine species and, as a more experienced hobbyist,

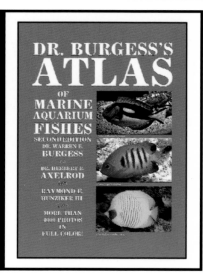

Containing more than 4000 full-color photos in its 768 pages, *Dr. Burgess's Atlas of Marine Aquarium Fishes* (T.F.H Publications style # H-1100) is the premier identification guide to saltwater aquarium fishes of all kinds.

expand the number and types of species you can care for.

A sampling of beginners' fishes is just that, a sampling. Your future favorite might not be listed here, and you may despise one which is listed. You will not find Moorish idols here, or any other high-priced, hard-to-keep species. Tangs are omitted, despite their frequent appearance in dealers' tanks, since they will fare better in the tanks of more experienced hobbyists. Butterflyfishes and angelfishes, though gorgeous, are not listed, since you should wait a little while before taking on these more difficult species. Sharks, rays, moray eels, and other titillating denizens of the deep are conspicuously absent, since these species are for a public aquarium or the tanks of an advanced marine aquarist. Even the snowflake moray, an otherwise easy-to-keep species, is going to present feeding and escape headaches you don't need the first time around.

Taken as a general guide, the suggestions here will get you pointed in the right direction, but the rules for husbandry already discussed in this book will serve you well for almost any fish you knowledgeably select from a reliable dealer's tank.

INVERTEBRATES

Whoa! Wasn't this **KISS** business founded on a fish-only premise? Well, yes, but...

You may find offered for sale various marine invertebrates that are actually suitable for your first tank. Some crustaceans (crabs, lobsters, and shrimp), for example, are hardy, colorful, interesting, and inexpensive. While many of them will prey on other invertebrates, most get along well with fishes large enough to avoid capture. In addition, they are excellent litter patrols, picking up any food particles the other tank inhabitants miss. A perennial favorite is the hermit crab, cousin of the popular terrestrial species.

Mollusks are generally a poor choice for your aquarium for a variety of reasons. Many of them are specialized feeders. With some it is difficult to tell if they are alive or not, and they can pollute a tank *fast* if their demise goes unnoticed. The squids and octopuses are predatory escape artists, who, if provoked, can poison everything in the tank, including themselves, with their defensive ink emissions. Some of them can even give you a nasty

Hermit crabs can be useful (and comical) additions to the aquarium, and some are colorful as well. Shown is a hermit crab of the genus *Pagurus*.

PHOTO BY COURTNEY PLATT.

Turbo snails, useful for their tendency to graze upon algae that forms on surfaces within the aquarium.

PHOTO BY MARK SMITH.

Certain snails can be useful in keeping down unwanted algal growth, and they and their shell-less cousins the nudibranchs can be flamboyantly colorful. Some of those beautiful nudibranchs, however, are very predatory, with a few of them specialized to feed on other nudibranchs, and some cone snails are so venomous that they have been featured as the murder weapon in baffling whodunits.

It is best to restrict your first invertebrates to a small crab or shrimp or two. Cleaner shrimps, which are highly colored to advertise their don't-eat-me role as parasite pickers, may even indulge in that behavior if you house them with compatible fishes. A good rule of thumb is to

venomous bite. The octopuses are also highly intelligent and dexterous, able to learn to uncork bottles and open hatches to get food. Think what their eight flexible and muscular arms can do to your filter, heater, hood, etc.

Sepia officinalis, the common cuttlefish, in a defensive pose—and anything that could throw this highly skilled predator into a defensive posture must be menacing indeed. Cuttlfishes are even less suitable for inclusion in a beginner's tank than their molluskan relatives the octopuses and the squids.

PHOTO BY RAY HUNZIKER.

Beginners often are tempted into acquiring nudibranchs like this *Flabellina iodinea* because of their colorfulness and bizarre shapes—but they're better left out of the aquaria of inexperienced owners.

PHOTO BY COURTNEY PLATT.

The beautiful cleaner shrimp *Lysmata amboinensis*. Be careful not to house this species or any other delicate crustacean with fishes (or anything else) that can easily make a meal out of them.

PHOTO BY MP AND C. PIEDNOIR, AQUA PRESS.

assume your crustaceans are extremely territorial and to limit them to one of a species per tank, even though a few of them get along well communally. Almost all of them are cave or burrow dwellers, so plenty of nooks and crannies are important, especially so that they can hide safely after molting, before their new exoskeleton hardens.

There are several species of shrimps that form commensal symbiotic relationships with certain hardy goby/blenny species. The excavating shrimp houses and scavenges after the goby, who serves as an early warning against predators as well as grocery deliverer; the shrimp feeds off the table scraps of its host/guest. Such a pair makes for

Above: *Amblyeleotris guttata,* one of the goby species that typically live in symbiotic associations with "snapping" shrimp of the family Alphaeidae, such as *Alphaeus normani,* below. Upper photo: Roger Steene; lower photo: Alex Kerstitch.

Anemones and starfish can make immensely interesting additions to a marine aquarium, but beginners should put off their acquisition until they get more experience in the hobby.

PHOTO BY DR. HERBERT R. AXELROD.

some fascinating inhabitants of a marine tank, as long as you get compatible species.

If you make a limited venture into the invertebrate side of the hobby, you can stay within **KISS** limitations and still enjoy a smidgen of the non-fish inhabitants of the ocean. Leave the live corals, anemones, sea squirts, feather worms, and starfish for your first reef tank, sometime down the road.

DAMSELFISHES

Damselfishes (family Pomacentridae) are the guppies of the saltwater hobby in the sense that they are the first fish for many aquarists—easy to keep, colorful, interesting—and even one of the types of marine fishes already bred in captivity. People who start with damsels often continue in the hobby.

In fact, like experienced and jaded freshwater hobbyists who "rediscover" guppies, many marine aquarists buy a group of hardy damsels to cycle a new tank, but by the time the biofilter is operating, they've become enamored of them and don't want to part with them.

Damsels are custom-made beginner fishes. They come in a

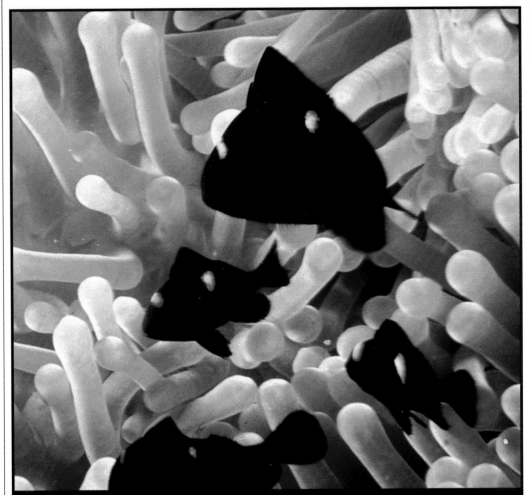

The three-spot damselfish, *Dascyllus trimaculatus,* one of the popular stand-bys of the marine fish trade. Like their cousins the clownfishes, a number of *Dascyllus* species also are at home in anemones, although they occupy the anemones over shorter periods of time.

PHOTO BY MP AND C. PIEDNOIR, AQUA PRESS.

wide variety of colors and patterns, from black and white, either spots or stripes, to brilliant solid colors, including several bright blue species commonly called "blue devils." They are undemanding, hardy, and eager feeders—something that cannot be said for many other marine species. Just about their only drawback is their territoriality, a problem with most species of damselfishes.

Some hobbyists recommend having just one individual of several species, since intraspecific aggression is usually the worst. By choosing dissimilar-looking species, you can avoid a lot of the territorial battling. Another technique, also used by African rift lake cichlid hobbyists, is to keep several of a given species, which actually diminishes the aggression by diffusing each agonistic act among many targets.

The damselfishes in general are territorial and combative, but many also are very colorful or at least attractively marked. This is *Pomacentrus vaiuli,* exhibiting a color pattern more or less the reverse of that displayed by another damselfish, *Chrysiptera hemicyanea,* shown below.

PHOTOS BY DR. GERALD R. ALLEN.

Dascyllus melanurus, a very hardy damselfish and one of the best fishes for a beginner's first aquarium.

PHOTO BY U. ERICH FRIESE

Often a fish is so busy watching over its shoulder (dorsal fin?) for the next attack that it doesn't launch one of its own.

By starting with a group of small fish and providing plenty of cover and room for territories, you should be successful in achieving a suitable if tense harmony. Adding a new fish to a tankful of damsels is, however, like adding a match to a keg of dynamite. If you must do it, take out all the decorations, mix them up to dissolve territory boundary markers, and preferably place more than one newcomer at a time.

ANEMONEFISHES

Anemonefishes, which include the stereotypical marine aquarium fish, the clownfish, are specialized damselfishes that have adapted to life within the nematocyst-armed tentacles of the deadly (to most other fishes) sea anemones. Not only are clownfish hardy, fairly easy to breed, and fascinatingly colorful, they also are always a hit as they nestle among the stinging anemone's waving limbs.

The commensalism between the clownfish and its host anemone is one of the better-known wonders of the coral reef, familiar even to some people who know nothing else about marine life. The temptation to get a pair of clowns and a colorful anemone will be great, but you *must* resist.

Anemones are not KISSable, no matter how hard you try. They are

A fully adult clownfish enfolding itself within the tenacles of its host anemone. There are two genera of clownfishes, *Amphiprion* and *Premnas,* and not all of them exhibit the typical "clown" markings. This is *Premnas biaculeatus.*

PHOTO BY MP AND C. PIEDNOIR, AQUA PRESS.

The clownfish *Amphiprion ocellaris* having a confrontation with an equally colorful and similarly marked—and named—wrasse, *Coris gaimard,* the clown wrasse.

PHOTO BY DR. KARL KNAACK.

among those invertebrates that need all that fancy expensive lighting. They are among those invertebrates that are particularly fussy about water conditions. They are hard to feed properly. For a beginner they are trouble just waiting to happen. They also smell incredibly bad when they die and start turning into a slimy goo in your tank.

This does not mean that you have to give up your clownfish, however. While they seem happier, and some people feel they are healthier, with a nice anemone to come home to, they will survive and even thrive without one. And while they normally spawn in or near their host anemone, clownfishes are even bred commercially like cichlids—one pair per bare tank, with a flat spawning surface. Captive-bred clownfishes are available and worth the higher price they may carry.

CAN'T I KEEP SOME ANGELS?

Between size constraints and feeding problems, most angelfishes and butterflyfishes would be excluded from your **KISS** tank, even if they weren't quarrelsome and scrappy. Unfortunately, the husbandry problems associated with many of these species are equally matched by their outrageously gorgeous coloration. All is not lost, however, because there are many beautiful but peaceful dwarf or pygmy angels, of the genus *Centropyge*, that are possible candidates for your first marine tank.

You can choose from many species of beautifully colored three- to six-inch pygmy angels, from the peacock purple, gold, and green *C. bispinosus* to the blue and yellow *C. acanthops*, to the pure yellow *C. heraldi* or the yellow *C. flavissimus*, which adds blue "eye makeup" and gill and fin

Centropyge flavissimus.

PHOTO BY DR. KARL KNAACK.

A juvenile *Centropyge acanthops.*

PHOTO BY JOACHIM FRISCHE.

edges, to various barred and solid and bicolor species.

All of these species are grazers, some being totally herbivorous, but algae and green foods are a lot easier to supply than the living sponges many larger angels require. Most of the pygmy angels will also accept meaty foods. Though not as hardy as some of the larger species, and perhaps better saved for later on in your first tank, after you have a bit of experience, these fishes are nevertheless relatively undemanding, and they're a nice step up in challenge from the "cast iron" damselfishes.

GROUPERS

You are probably familiar with the giant groupers that greet

Centropyge bicolor.

PHOTO BY DR. KARL KNAACK.

Centropyge bispinosus.

PHOTO BY KEN LUCAS.

Centropyge heraldi.

PHOTO BY U. ERICH FRIESE.

similar-sized scuba divers. There are a few species from the grouper and sea bass family that are small enough for large aquaria, such as *Grammistes sexlineatus*, which has many (more than six) white lines on its dark body that turn to rows of dotted lines as they mature.

Baby panther groupers, *Cromileptes altivelis*, are commonly offered for sale, and they are irresistibly patterned, with terrific personalities. Their adult size of two to three feet, however, should give you pause as you gaze longingly into your dealer's tank.

More suitable are the dwarf relatives of the groupers, the fairy basslets, grammas, and

Cromileptes altivelis on the prowl for something to eat.

PHOTO BY MP. AND C. PIEDNOIR, AQUA PRESS.

Grammistes sexlineatus. Although it's far from being in a class with some of the other groupers as far as size is concerned, the golden-striped grouper can probably match some of the big boys in the appetite department; it is a very heavy feeder and not trustworthy around smaller fishes.

PHOTO BY MP. AND C. PIEDNOIR, AQUA PRESS.

Pseudochromis paccagnellae.

PHOTO BY JOHN O'MALLEY.

dottybacks. Two stunning species are *Pseudochromis paccagnellae* and *Gramma loreto*, both of which are magenta in front and orange in back. They are hardy and beautiful, but often extremely quarrelsome and territorial. They cannot be kept with their own kind or species of similar habits, though one of them in a mixed-species tank is a real show-stopper.

Gramma loreto.

PHOTO BY KLAUS PAYSAN.

Neocirrhites armatus, commonly called the flame hawkfish.

PHOTO BY KEN LUCAS.

The longnosed hawkfish, *Oxycirrhites typus,* is a relatively peaceul aquarium resident but sure death to any small crustaceans in its tank.

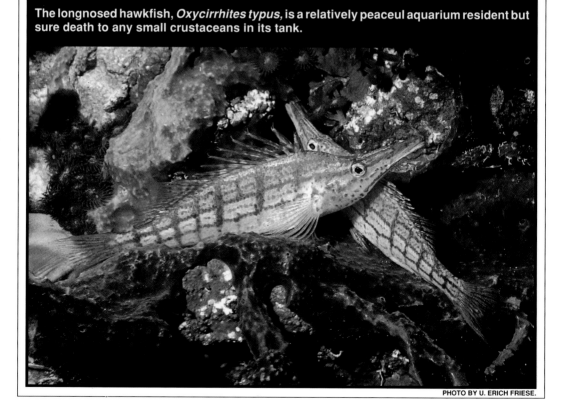

PHOTO BY U. ERICH FRIESE.

OTHER GOOD THINGS IN SMALL PACKAGES

There are other tiny gems suitable for your **KISS** tank. These include the hawkfishes (*Neocirrhites* or *Oxycirrhites*), which perch on a piece of coral or rock like a bird of prey waiting to swoop down on its dinner as it swims below.

Various gobies have the distinction of being small, hardy, extremely colorful, and peaceful. Included would be the neon goby, *Gobiosoma oceanops*. A bright display can be set up with a variety of small gobies.

Similarly, many of the smaller wrasses, such as the cleaner wrasse, *Labroides dimidatus*, and the reindeer wrasse, *Novaculichthys taeniourus*, are peaceful additions to the community setting.

BLENNIES

The diminutive blennies deserve separate mention, since they have unique assets and liabilities. They are extremely hardy and, like most other bottom dwelling fishes with reduced swim bladders, comically interesting. They are also some of those "personality" fishes that endear themselves to their owners with such things as eating out of their hands. Some of them are quite colorful, though not matching the neon elegance of many other marine tropicals.

So what's wrong with them? They can be very territorial, and some are quite predatory (as for example *Aspidontous taeniatus*, a mimic of the cleaner wrasse that, instead of picking parasites off the unwitting patron, takes a chunk of its flesh!), so while a mixed group of blennies is possible, you

Gobiosoma oceanops, the neon goby, whose common name obviously derives from the electric-blue lateral stripe.

PHOTO BY WALTER A. STARCK II.

Aspidontus taeniatus is a sneaky little blenny that imitates the appearance of the cleaner wrasse *Labroides dimidiatus* (below) and feeds off the unsuspecting clients who present themselves for being cleaned of parasites.

UPPER PHOTO BY DR. HERBERT R. AXELROD; LOWER PHOTO BY H. HANSEN.

Novaculichthys taeniourus, the reindeer wrasse. This is a young specimen; an older fish would be much less frilled.

must be careful in selecting tankmates for them. They also are crevice-dwellers that become tense and stressed if kept without shelter but often invisible if provided with appropriate hidey holes. The latter defect can be overcome by their voracious appetites, but between feedings their aquarium may get a bit boring to watch.

NIGHT LIFE

Several largely nocturnal species, with the concomitant extra-large eyes, are hardy and suitable for the **KISS** tank, most notably the cardinalfishes (family Apongonidae), which are timid and need to have sedate tankmates, and the squirrelfishes (family Holocentridae), which are boisterous and active (though not so much through the day), and are poor companions for retiring species such as the cardinalfishes.

If acclimated gradually to a brighter and brighter tank, and if provided with plenty of daytime hiding spots and caves, and if they are fed during the day, these interesting mostly red fishes will adjust to a less nocturnal lifestyle.

"EQUINES"

Seahorses and the related pipefishes are very interesting and

Apogon pseudomaculatus, showing the relatively large eyes characteritic of the cardinalfishes in general.

PHOTO BY DR. KARL KNAACK.

Pterapogon kauderni, a very distinctively marked cardinalfish species.

PHOTO BY MARK SMITH.

Like the cardinalfishes, the squirrelfishes also have relatively large eyes; this squirrelfish is *Holocentrus rufus.*

PHOTO BY DR. GERALD R. ALLEN.

unusual creatures, unique among vertebrates in that the male is the one who gets pregnant. In a big turnaround of normal procreation, the female oviposits into the male's brood sac, where the eggs are fertilized and where they develop until they are born, literally expelled by muscular contractions from their father's "womb." Decades ago I witnessed this as a child, in an aquarium shop in Manhattan, and to this day I marvel at the memory of that male fish in labor, expelling stream after stream of "seafoals" with strenuous spasms.

Vertical seahorses and their horizontal cousins the pipefishes are not really beginners' fishes if they have to be kept in mixed company. But alone in their own aquarium, seahorses can be suitable for your first tank. They are not primarily reef dwellers like other marine tropicals, but live even far out to sea, sucking in live prey as it swims or floats by their handy perches among the seaweed. The frenetic, bustling activity of many reef fishes is intolerable for them, and in such a situation the seahorses would get nothing to eat. They require peace and quiet, without competition from more boisterous types, but you can keep a "herd" of them together.

The most difficult part of keeping seahorses is keeping

Small-mouthed and non-aggressive like their seahorse cousins, the pipefishes also share the seahorses' characteristic of having the males carry the eggs. This male *Syngnathus biaculeatus* has developing eggs visible at his abdominal area.

PHOTO BY MP. AND C. PIEDNOIR, AQUA PRESS.

them fed, since their food should be continuously available, small, and alive. Smaller seahorses can subsist on brine shrimp nauplii, but be careful not to introduce any eggshells, as they are implicated in often-fatal digestive problems. Larger specimens will also eat baby brine shrimp, as well as adult shrimp, daphnia, and baby livebearers.

Seahorses come in a wide variety of colors and sizes— black, white, and even bright yellow, red, or orange— and if you can provide a separate tank with suitable perches onto which the seahorses can lash their prehensile tails, and plenty of live food willing to swim or drift past the perching seahorses and get sucked into their tubular snouts, and a filtration system that will not strain out the food organisms

before the horses can get them, you can enjoy the lazy antics of these fascinating fish.

SEA COWS?

Cowfishes and other boxfishes are related to puffers and porcupinefishes (see "Familiar Friends" below). These unlikely-looking creatures are peaceful and interesting aquarium residents, but when disturbed they produce a toxic substance that can poison any of the tank inhabitants, including themselves! Transporting these fishes is therefore a tricky business, though once established in a tank they are not too easily provoked. Although their main appeal is their unusual appearance, they are hardy, KISSable pets. A popular species is the aptly named *Lactoria cornuta*, or "horned milker."

Seahorses are peaceful and hardy if you can provide them with the food they need and can arrange to make sure that they're able to capture it, but they'd starve to death in a mixed community of fishes. The species shown is *Hippocampus erectus*.

PHOTO BY J. KELLY GIWOJNA.

The cowfish *Lactoria cornuta.*

PHOTO BY DR. HERBERT R. AXELROD.

TOXIC TURKEYS

Staying with the unusual, fish of the genera *Pterois* and *Dendrochirus*, known as lionfishes, scorpion fishes, or turkeyfishes, are beautiful but deadly marine tropicals. The venom in their spines is toxic enough that you should not attempt to see how resistant you are to it. The fishes themselves, however, make good aquarium inhabitants, and they are even appropriate for a community tank in which none of the other residents is small enough to be swallowed, since although live fishes are the lionfishes' preferred fare, they are not otherwise aggressive.

Like many other venomous creatures, they are strikingly colored; again like many other venomous creatures, they are placid and easygoing, able to be kept in mixed or single-species groups. Who needs to be bossy when anyone attacking will inject himself with venom?

Obviously, you should be extremely careful when moving a lionfish or when maintaining an aquarium containing one. No matter how tame it is, do not trust the fish and stick your hand into the tank without placing some sort of partition (a rectangle of plastic "egg crate" light diffuser works well) between it and the area you need to service. And, of course, the tank needs to be positioned and covered in such a way that children cannot gain access to it. In general, toxic pets

With all of its frills and banners waving, this *Pterois lunulata* lionfish is almost as elegant as it is venomous.

PHOTO BY MICHAEL DEFREITAS.

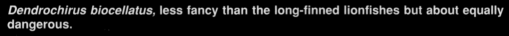

Dendrochirus biocellatus, less fancy than the long-finned lionfishes but about equally dangerous.

PHOTO BY K.H. CHOO.

Antennarius biocellatus, one of the anglerfishes, so named because they dangle a fleshy bait from their bodies to lure intended victims into engulfing range.

PHOTO BY K.H. CHOO.

Closeup of the head area of a species of *Synanceja,* one of the big-mouthed and venomous stonefishes.

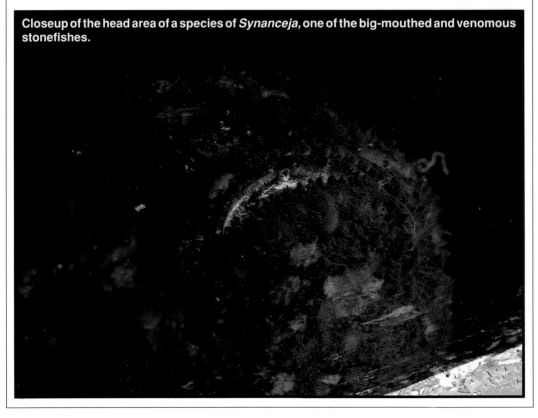

of any type are not recommended for households with children younger than adolescent.

At a marine theme park aquarium I've seen a tall cylindrical tank teeming with lionfishes— several hundred of them. Being inquisitive and tame, almost all of them were oriented to the front of the tank, watching the people watching them. It made a very impressive display.

Looking into the business end of the lionfish *Pterois volitans* is the last thing many a small fish will ever do.

PHOTO BY MP. AND C. PIEDNOIR, AQUA PRESS.

TOXIC UGLIES

Some other poisonous and/or grotesque species are sometimes kept by hobbyists. The stonefishes, toadfishes, and anglerfishes (frogfishes) are hardy although "cosmetically challenged." They make unusually hardy and interesting pets, but all of them have BIG mouths, and some of them are able to engulf fishes almost the same size as they are, so they will quickily turn a community tank into a single-fish tank. And beware of the venomous spines on the stonefishes and toadfishes!

MANDARINS

As tiny, beautiful, and inoffensive as the stonefishes are big, ugly, and dangerous, mandarins (genus *Synchiropus)* are hardy, very colorful, and comical fishes. They usually do not get along well with their own kind and therefore should be kept singly or as a pair if you can get an established pair. They are bottom-hugging and fairly inactive, and they require non-boisterous tankmates. These traits make them one of the few species you might be able to keep with seahorses.

JAWFISHES

Fish of the genus *Opisthognathus* are sometimes available. Many of these unusual fishes are seen normally only from the gills up, as they keep the rest of their body in their home burrows in the sand. At any sign

Synchiropus splendidus indeed embodies somebody's notion of splendor as it sails slowly through its mini-reef tank home.

PHOTO BY MP. AND C. PIEDNOIR, AQUA PRESS.

A little less fancy in its dress than *Synchiropus splendidus* but just s desirable as an inhabitant of a mini-reef aquarium is *S. picturatus.*

PHOTO BY DR. HERBERT R. AXELROD.

Opisthognathus aurifrons, the pearly jawfish, popping out of a hole it has constructed for itself in the substrate.

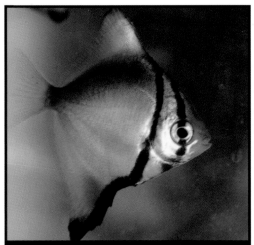

Monodactylus argenteus individuals switched from fresh to salt water should be acclimated slowly.

PHOTO BY M.H. SHARP.

of danger, they retreat backwards into their holes. They are peaceful, with other fishes and with others of their own species, as long as there is sufficient room for each to have its own burrow. As for most nervous, timid fishes, the jawfishes' tankmates must be chosen with care to avoid their being intimidated or harassed.

FAMILIAR FRIENDS AND THEIR RELATIVES

Familiar fishes you already are acquainted with may be suitable for your marine tank. The list includes puffers, monos, and

Scatophagus argus, another popular aquarium fish that can adapt to freshwater and marine habitats.

PHOTO BY H.J. RICHTER.

scats. Some of these fishes are found in a variety of habitats, from fresh through brackish to even full seawater; with suitably gradual acclimatization, they can go into your saltwater aquarium. While these species usually do not thrive in straight fresh water, they do very well in salt water.

Also, saltwater relatives of familiar freshwater species are available. Most gobies are marine, as discussed above, but some of the brackish species are common in the freshwater hobby, so you may already know this interesting and comical group of fishes.

If you want to keep puffers, there are several more species to choose from than are available in fresh (brackish) dealer's tanks, but remember that many species are nasty, and all are equipped with a substantial biting beak.

Add spines to the inflatable puffers and you get porcupine-fish, hardy and fascinating pets that need a tank of their own, which many provide not only for the porcupine-fishes' unusual appearance but also for their cichlid-like tameness and their awareness and appreciation of the hand that feeds them.

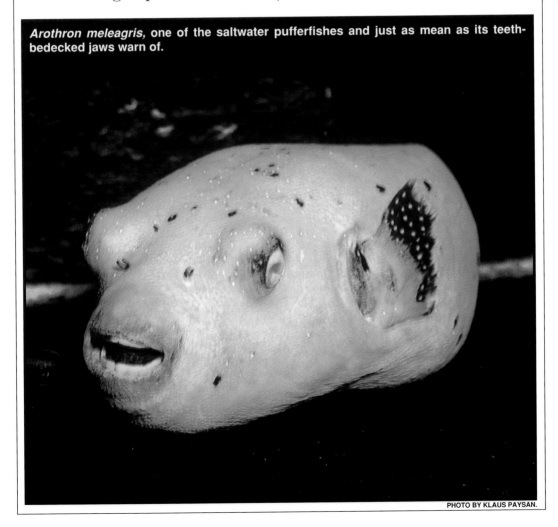

Arothron meleagris, **one of the saltwater pufferfishes and just as mean as its teeth-bedecked jaws warn of.**

PHOTO BY KLAUS PAYSAN.

A *Diodon* species, one of the porcupinefishes, so called because of the "quills" that stick out of them.

PHOTO BY JOHN O'MALLEY.

The catfish *Arius jordani.*

PHOTO BY GLEN S. AXELROD.

Plotosus lineatus, as per usual in a big group; single specimens are almost never encountered in the wild.

PHOTO BY WALT DEAS.

The catfishes of the genus *Arius,* often sold as a freshwater fish, is actually a brackish species, and the adults are fully marine. Also available in pet shops is the black and white striped bumblebee cat, *Plotosus lineatus,* a hectically active, schooling fish that should be kept in a group of six or more. A large swarm of these fish is a fascinating sight, not unlike a swarm of bees, so that even though they grow quite large and lose their striking coloration, they are popular as juveniles. The common name is quite appropriate, since aside from its appearance, *Plotosus* can deliver a venomous sting from its spines. The sting can prove fatal, so handle them with care.

Strictly carnivorous species whose usual means of feeding is to swallow their prey whole, such as this *Pterois antennata,* often will accept only living fishes as food, but most marine aquarium species learn to eagerly accept commercially prepared aquarium foods in a number of different forms.

PHOTO BY MP. AND C. PIEDNOIR, AQUA PRESS.

FEEDING YOUR MARINE FISHES

Feeding marine fishes is not much different from feeding freshwater fishes. Very small feedings of a variety of high-quality foods will provide your pets with the nutrition they need while preventing problems from decomposition of uneaten food.

The problem comes in getting the fishes to eat, something freshwater hobbyists have not had to deal with very often for decades now. There are many commercial flake and pellet foods formulated for the specific dietary needs of marine fishes, but many species need the coaxing of frozen, if not living, food organisms. While freshwater organisms can be useful in feeding marine tropicals, they must be balanced with marine foods, since certain fatty acids are missing in freshwater species. A steady diet of goldfish, for example, will leave you with a malnourished lionfish, and marine baitfish or pieces of a saltwater fish are a much better choice.

Many marines need vegetable matter in their diet, and you can supplement the algae that will naturally grow in your tank with blanched fresh vegetables such as zucchini slices or peas. There are also excellent commercial preparations for herbivorous species, many based on the highly nutritious *Spirulina* algae.

There are many recipes in the literature for homemade concoctions for marine fishes, most of which are quite nourishing and suitable, but none of which are necessary, plus they are not at all KISSable. There is

Frozen foods are convenient to use and eaten with gusto by marine aquarium inhabitants, making them practical to use also. Photo courtesy of Ocean Nutrition.

Flake foods based on Spirulina algae are especially suitable for tangs and other fishes heavily dependent on foods with a high vegetable content, but other species benefit from them as well. Spirulina algae also stimulate fishes' immune systems to attack disease-causing bacteria. Photo courtesy of Ocean Star International.

no need for you to mess up your kitchen and make your blender all slimy with raw seafood just to feed your pets. With the plethora of frozen and prepared marine diets commercially available, the only concern you will have is with those fishes that simply will not accept non-living prey. Even these fishes, however, can usually in time be trained to take strips of fish dangled or twitched in front of their noses.

Whatever foods you use, remember that while overfeeding a freshwater tank is bad, overfeeding a marine aquarium can be even more quickly fatal. In addition, many species can grow too large for captivity, and sparse feeding keeps them growing at a slower pace.

Pelleted foods are available in a wide variety of ingredients, so hobbyists are able to offer their fishes a diet that contains a full range of nutritional elements. Photo courtesy of Ocean Star International.

HEALTH CONCERNS

PREVENTION

The old adage is right: a pound of cure is the cost of forgetting your ounce of prevention. In addition, when we're talking about marine fishes, that pound of cure is quite likely to be ineffective, and then the lives of your aquarium's inhabitants can be the cost. So make positive, proactive health practices part of your daily fish maintenance program, and you will avoid most problems.

We've already covered many of these practices—water changes, proper filtration, stocking rates, proper feeding. Also important is intense observation of your fishes, something you undoubtedly will be doing anyway, but be alert to subtle changes in appearance and behavior that can signal illness. Healthy fishes are hungry fishes, and any fish that refuses to eat needs careful watching. This brings up the importance of carefully selecting your fishes in the first place.

SELECTION AND QUARANTINE

As with freshwater fishes, you should inspect any potential purchases, plus the other fishes in the tank with them, for signs of illness or injury. Everything you are used to looking for in freshwater specimens applies here: avoid white spots, red spots, bruises, open sores, heavy breathing, cottony growths,

listlessness, and erratic swimming. These last two need a qualification. Marine fishes have evolved a wide variety of locomotory patterns. The hopping of a goby, the hovering of a cowfish, or the dorsal fin ruddering of a seahorse are all unusual, but not for them! And many marine tropicals normally have their fins unextended, so be careful not to diagnose normal fin postures as "clamped fins." As always, your reputable dealer can help explain what is normal for the species you are considering.

In addition, since refusal to eat is a common problem in wild-caught marine tropicals, you should only purchase fishes that you have seen eating. Ask the dealer to feed the fish, and don't accept any excuses for why they aren't eating. If they won't take food, don't take them home. Leave the overcoming of hunger strikes to experienced hobbyists, most of whom won't undertake the task anyway.

Once you get your new pet home, do not put it into your community tank. Put it into a quarantine tank. I know, in the **KISS** paradigm we were talking about only one tank. You are always better off quarantining, but if you consider the very first couple of fish that were helping you cycle your biofilter as expendable, you can add the remaining fish and have just one fully stocked tank. But from that time on, if you contemplate getting any more fishes, you are by definition starting to expand your hobby, and you must buy at least two more tanks, the new one and a quarantine/hospital tank.

The quarantine tank can be small, say ten gallons. It can be minimally decorated, maybe just a hunk of PVC pipe for a hiding "cave." A bare bottom is useful for keeping it clean. For filtration, if you are only going to set it up on occasion when you buy fish, you can use a sponge filter, which you keep running in the corner of your main tank the rest of the time to keep the bacterial culture alive.

Keep your new fish in here for a month or longer, until you are certain it is free of parasites and disease, and until it has recovered from the shocks and traumas of being netted, shipped, and reshipped. This not only keeps the newcomer from infecting your healthy tank but also gets it into the best condition before it has to face its new, already established tankmates.

MEDICATIONS

When, despite your best precautions, your fish do fall ill to white spot (the saltwater "ich" caused by the protozoan *Cryptocaryon*) or some other malady, your dealer can help you in diagnosing and selecting treatment. The tried and true medication for saltwater fishes is copper, usually as copper sulfate. If you have invertebrates, remember that the lethal dose for

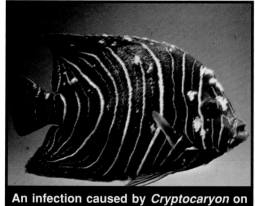

An infection caused by *Cryptocaryon* on an angelfish, *Pomacanthus semicirculatus*.

PHOTO BY FRICKHINGER.

them is about half the lethal dose for fishes, well within normal medication boundaries, and that for some inverts, *any* copper is deadly. There is also concern that copper will be taken up and stored in coral and sand, so a tank once treated with copper may never be able to be used for a reef tank without being totally cleaned and refitted with new materials.

Most medications disturb or destroy the bacteria in your biofilter as well, so treat a sick fish in a hospital tank if at all possible. That quarantine tank is perfect for this as well, but the biofilter will need to be regrown afterwards.

With reasonable vigilance and consistent preventive care, your fish should thrive under your care. You will enjoy them, and you will be gaining experience and knowledge. In a while, now that you've learned to **KISS**, you may be expanding your collection. In fact, you may start eyeing open spaces along your walls, wondering where to put that perfect reef tank.